THE FIVE SENSES OF THE ANIMAL WORLD

Touch

Text: Andreu Llamas
Illustrations: Francisco Arredondo

El tacto © Copyright EDICIONES ESTE, S. A., 1995, Barcelona, Spain

Touch Copyright © 1996 by Chelsea House Publishers, a division of Main Line Book Co. All rights reserved.

1 3 5 7 9 8 6 4 2

Library of Congress Cataloging-in-Publication Data

Llamas, Andreu.
 [Tacto. English]
 Touch / text, Andreu Llamas ; illustrations, Francisco Arredondo.
  p. cm. — (The Five senses of the animal world)
 Translation of El tacto.
 Includes index.
 Summary: Explains the sense of touch including information on the function of the skin, how the body measures and feels temperatures and how it responds to pain, and the sensitivity of whiskers.
 ISBN 0-7910-3494-1. — ISBN 0-7910-3499-2 (pbk.)
 1. Touch—Juvenile literature. [1. Touch. 2. Skin. 3. Senses and sensation.] I. Arredondo, Francisco, ill. II. Title. III. Series.
QP451.l6313 1996   95-14781
591.1'827—dc20   CIP
                                                   AC

Contents

What Is the Sense of Touch?	4
The Mystery of the Skin	6
Hot and Cold	8
Pain	10
Body Position	12
Waves in the Water	14
The Insects' Sense of Touch	16
Arthropod Skin	18
Sensitive Whiskers	20
The Sand Scorpions' Touch	22
Sensitive to the Force of Gravity	24
Other Special Sensitivities	26
How Spiders Detect Their Prey	28
The Electrical Sense	30
Glossary	32
Index	32

THE FIVE SENSES OF THE ANIMAL WORLD

Touch

CHELSEA HOUSE PUBLISHERS
New York • Philadelphia

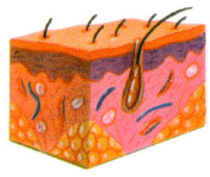

What Is the Sense of Touch?

The sense of touch is prevalent throughout the animal world because it provides information about objects that are in direct contact with the body.

This sense permits the animal to find out about an object's qualities just by touching it. The receptors that do this are called tactile receptors. They are made up of sensorial nerve cells that stretch from the skin cells to the mucous membranes. They are abundant on the body's surface and are responsible for the sensations of touch, heat, cold, and pain.

When an object touches the body, it produces pressure, causing an immediate change in the sensorial endings' shapes. This is how the tactile receptors are stimulated.

Touch allows an animal to know the shape, texture, size, and temperature of the objects it touches with its skin. There are two different types of nervous system receptors: the tactile *corpuscles* and the free nerve endings.

Some of these receptors are just nerve fiber endings and others are nerve endings encapsulated as corpuscles. The free nerve endings, for example, give us information about delicate or refined touch and the sense of pain.

Grandry's corpuscles can be found in birds' beaks.

Herbst's corpuscles can be found in birds' mouths and on exposed areas of their skin without a lot of feathers.

When a chimpanzee picks up a piece of fruit, it receives a lot of information: How much does it weigh? Is it fresh? Is it smooth? What shape does it have?

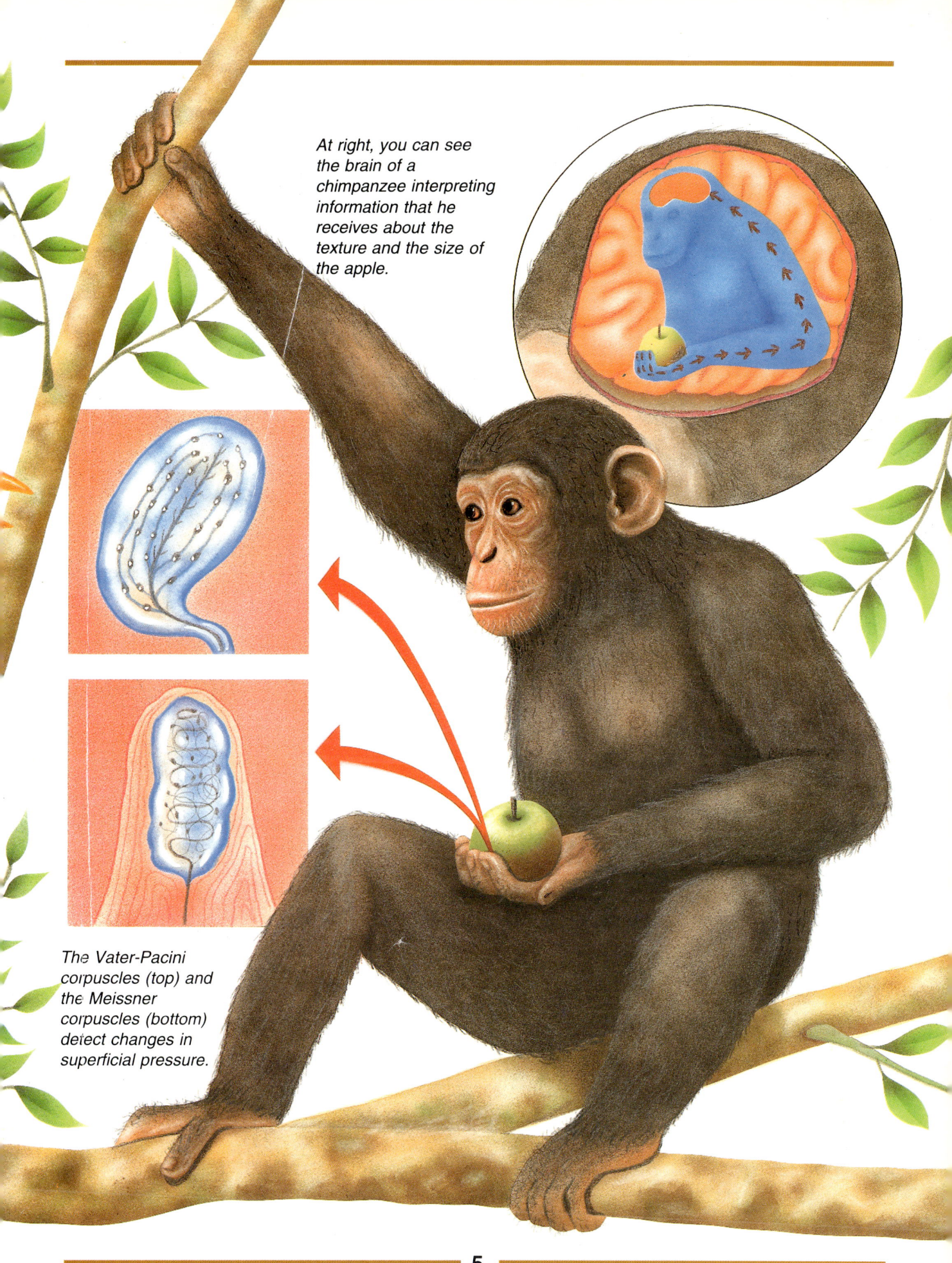

At right, you can see the brain of a chimpanzee interpreting information that he receives about the texture and the size of the apple.

The Vater-Pacini corpuscles (top) and the Meissner corpuscles (bottom) detect changes in superficial pressure.

The Mystery of the Skin

Skin is the organ in *vertebrates* that contains the nerve endings responsible for transmitting information received through the sense of touch.

In most animals, skin covers the entire body except for the natural orifices lined with mucous, such as the mouth. The skin has several different functions but the most important one is to protect and isolate the inside of an organism from the dangers of the outside world such as infections or loss of water. It is also very important for the skin to get information about the world that surrounds it. It can do this because of the sense of touch.

The skin is made up of three layers: the hypodermis, the dermis, and the epidermis. The hypodermis is the deepest layer of the skin and is mostly made up of fat. The dermis is the intermediate layer and is highly developed among mammals. It consists of a network of fibers spreading out in every direction. This is where some of the basic elements for the sense of touch can be found. The epidermis is the layer in direct contact with the outside world. It is made up of various layers of overlapping cells. Among these is the corneous layer, which serves as protection. In many animals, the corneous layer changes periodically like a continuously moving plate. In humans, however, small fragments of this layer, too small to be seen by the naked eye, fall off bit by bit.

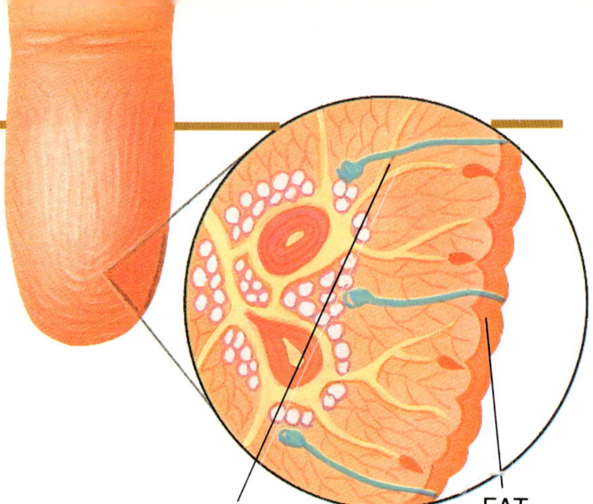

FREE NERVE ENDINGS

FAT

Mammals have a great quantity of free nerve endings in their fingertips.

Reptile skin has far fewer glands than amphibian or mammal skin. Its entire body is protected by a layer of strong scales that works like a barrier against the outside world.

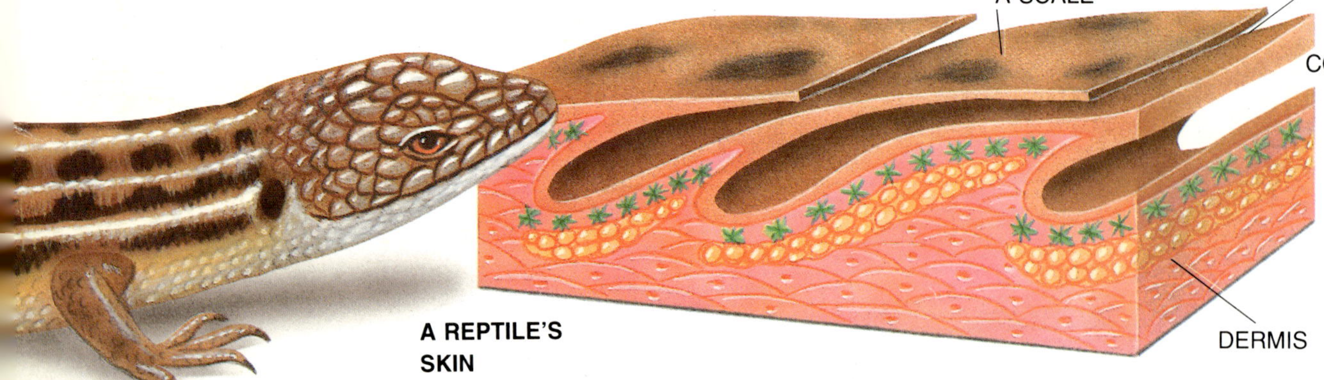

A SCALE

EPIDERMIS

CORNEOUS LAYER

DERMIS

A REPTILE'S SKIN

6

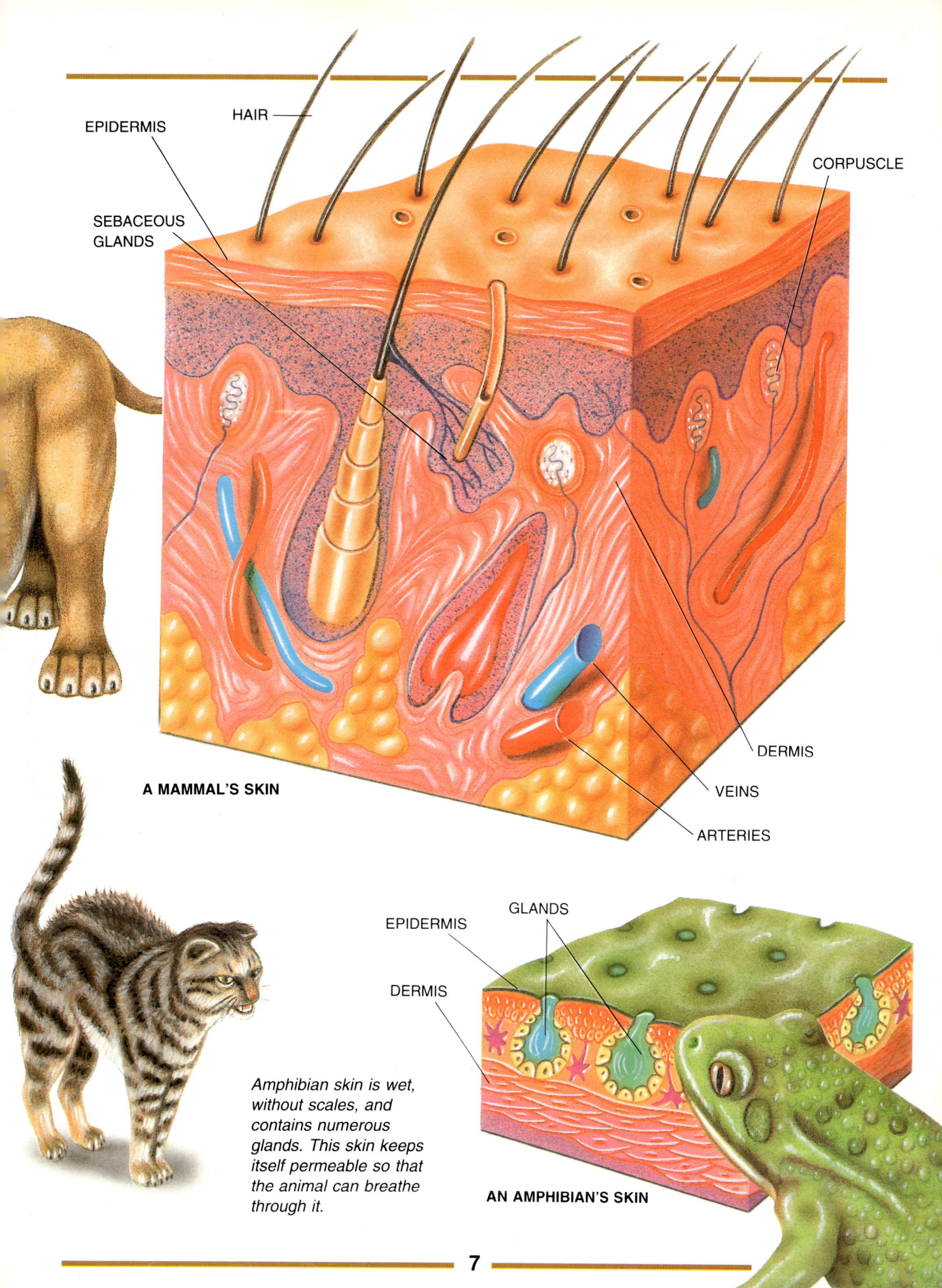

A MAMMAL'S SKIN

Amphibian skin is wet, without scales, and contains numerous glands. This skin keeps itself permeable so that the animal can breathe through it.

AN AMPHIBIAN'S SKIN

Hot and Cold

Have you ever wondered how the body measures and feels temperature?

Animals have receptors spread out all over their bodies that inform the brain about changes in their environment's temperature. This is very important because the vertebrates' differing activities are accomplished more efficiently at specific body temperatures. For the majority of animals it is absolutely fundamental to control their body temperature.

Temperature is measured inside the brain by a heat control center that works similar to a thermostat. When the brain gets a message saying, "too hot," the animal begins to sweat and pant. If it gets a message saying, "too cold," the animal's body begins to shiver.

When something inside the body is not working as it should, fever is usually one of the first symptoms that indicates that there is some sort of illness responsible.

In cold-blooded animals, such as reptiles, body temperature depends on their environment's temperature. For them, it is essential that they carefully choose where they live and the amount of hours they spend exposed to the sun. However, birds and mammals have good insulation (feathers, hair, and fat) that allows them to remain active even when it is very cold outside. These homeothermic animals have a structure (the hypothalamus, located in the brain stem) that regulates body temperature to keep it at the optimal level.

Here you can see a diagram showing how information about external temperature is transmitted from the peripheral receptors to the brain. The brain must interpret this information in order to be able to decide whether it should produce heat or lose it.

The terminal bulbs, or Krause's corpuscles, are considered to be the cold receptors because they are especially sensitive to low temperatures.

RUFFINI'S CORPUSCLES (HEAT RECEPTORS)

The terminal organs, or Ruffini's corpuscles, are considered to be the heat receptors. They are located at a much deeper layer within the dermis than the cold receptors and are sensitive to increases in temperature.

KRAUSE'S CORPUSCLES (COLD RECEPTORS)

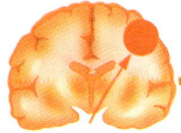

Pain

Have you ever pricked your finger with a needle? You probably moved your finger away as fast as possible, right?

You did this because the pain message did not reach your brain. It got as far as the *spinal cord*, which sent the order, "Move your finger away right now!" When something causing pain attacks the body, the organism responds with a reflex action. That is why when a painful sensation reaches the brain, the defensive response has already been generated in order to save valuable time.

The nerve receptors that inform us about a painful sensation consist of bare nerve endings that can be found in the deepest layers of the epidermis. They can also be found at the corneous layer, which does not contain any touch receptors.

Animals' bodies also have a system for detecting when something is not working correctly inside its body. These are the internal pain sensations that depend on receptors made up of free nerve endings found among the muscular fibers. Scientists believe that Pacini's corpuscles also transmit internal pain sensations. These corpuscles can be found in the mesenteries, the membranous layers covering the organs.

When the pain receptors detect an aggression, as in the above picture, the message to "move away" travels to the muscles from the spinal cord without having to go through the brain first.

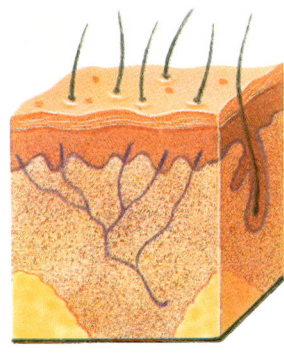

This is what the free nerve endings that carry the sensations of pain and delicate touch look like.

Being able to feel pain could mean the difference between life and death. When two male lions fight (1), the weaker one can feel the pain in the wounds that its powerful adversary inflicts (2). It can then decide to retreat to safety (3). If the two lions are an equal match, however, it is possible for one of the combatants to die.

Body Position

Why don't we fall out of bed while we're sleeping?

For animals it is very important to always know the exact position of all the body's different parts. The way to get all this information is through some very special receptors, called autoreceptors, located in the tendons, joints, and skeletal muscles. Thanks to these receptors, the brain receives constant information about the position and movement of the different parts of the body.

This peculiar sense of touch is called the autoreceptive sense and is especially important while the animal is asleep because it cannot consciously control its body position. This sense plays an important role among the five senses. Skin is capable of reporting where it is feeling pressure, the distance between two different stimuli, the shape and configuration of the object it is touching and whether or not the object is moving over its surface. As you can see, autoreceptors send a very different kind of internal message that helps complement the messages sent by the skin.

The shape of these autoreceptors is varied and can consist of free nerve endings or different types of spindles or corpuscles.

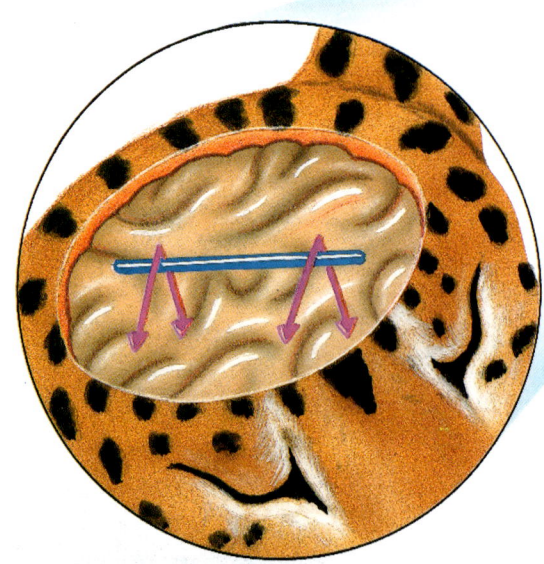

Animals change their body's position constantly while they are sleeping to avoid cramps and a feeling of restlessness. Furthermore, the brain (below) controls the position to avoid falls.

While an animal is sleeping, its perception of its surroundings is greatly reduced because its defense mechanisms have been turned off. This can have serious consequences because the animal's enemies could attack it before having time to react.

Knowing exactly how all the different parts of the body are positioned is the function of the autoreceptive sense and can be of vital importance to the animal, such as this squirrel.

The food koalas eat is so poor in nutritional value that they spend 18 hours per day sleeping on a branch. Thanks to the information that they get from the autoreceptors, they can be certain of not falling.

Before falling asleep or waking up, animals tend to stretch and yawn just like this gorilla.

13

Waves in the Water

There are many kinds of aquatic invertebrates that are very sensitive to small changes in hydrostatic pressure, or aquatic waves.

This type of sensitivity is very useful. The aquatic whirligigs, for example, provoke a whole series of waves when they move. Invertebrates have learned to detect and interpret the echoes that these waves make and create a picture of their surroundings, and some, like water bugs or water spiders, use aquatic waves for hunting. The water spider props its legs on the water to find its prey. It has little hairs on its legs that are very sensitive to even the smallest change on the water's surface. Every fish provokes its own particular wave while swimming. When it is a part of a *school* of fish and after it has established its position relative to the other fish, it uses its eyes and its lateral line to measure its companions' speed. By doing this it can maintain its position even in the dark. The lateral line is a very complicated organ that measures the speed of the water flowing over the fish, as well as its own speed.

If a shark suddenly attacks a school of fish, in just a fraction of a second all the fish can take off in opposite directions away from their attacker. They instantly break up the school but not one fish crashes into another. Afterward, the fish slowly join up again. This is impossible without the sense of touch provided by the lateral line.

The waves provoked by the whirligigs' movements come back to them as echoes that help them picture an image of the world around them.

1. The barracuda approaches to attack a school of fish but its movement makes waves that the fish's lateral lines can detect.

2. In less than a second, all the little fish have scattered in different directions.

3. When the danger is over, the fish form their school again.

The water bug that you can see moving on a puddle reacts very quickly when it detects possible prey like this fly that has fallen into the water.

The Insects' Sense of Touch

The insects' sense of touch is interesting because of the large number and variety of receptors that each insect has.

The simplest type of insect receptor is the sensorial hair. If you look carefully at an insect, you will notice a large number of little hairs on different parts of its body. These are simple and isolated sensorial organs that are always located on the body's *cuticle* and appendages. Their function is to capture the stimuli coming from both inside and outside the insect.

The insect's receptors have many important functions. Besides helping feel the tactile sensations, they also are related to the insect's orientation to gravity, the detection of vibrations coming from the *substrata* (both from the ground and water), and the vibrations sent through the air.

There are other much more complicated receptors that function to detect other types of vibrations. Some play a role in the insect's balance, some register the air's movements, and others function as auditory organs. In all of these instances, these receptors are deep sensorial organs that are distributed among the antennae, feelers, wings, legs, and thorax.

Insects also have autoreceptive organs (which inform the insect about its body position) that are stimulated by the pressures and tensions originating from inside the animal's body.

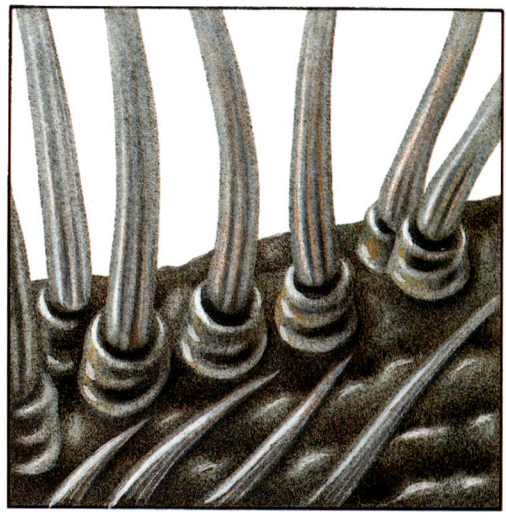

Here you can see the complicated little hairs all around the mouth of this carpet bug larva. Each hair has a joint at the base and is sensitive to vibrations.

This is what a hair on an insect's antenna looks like when amplified by an electron microscope.

The sense of touch is possible thanks to sensitive hairs that are spread out over different points of the body and the antennae. These tactile hairs are stimulated by the movement of the hair relative to the articular base.

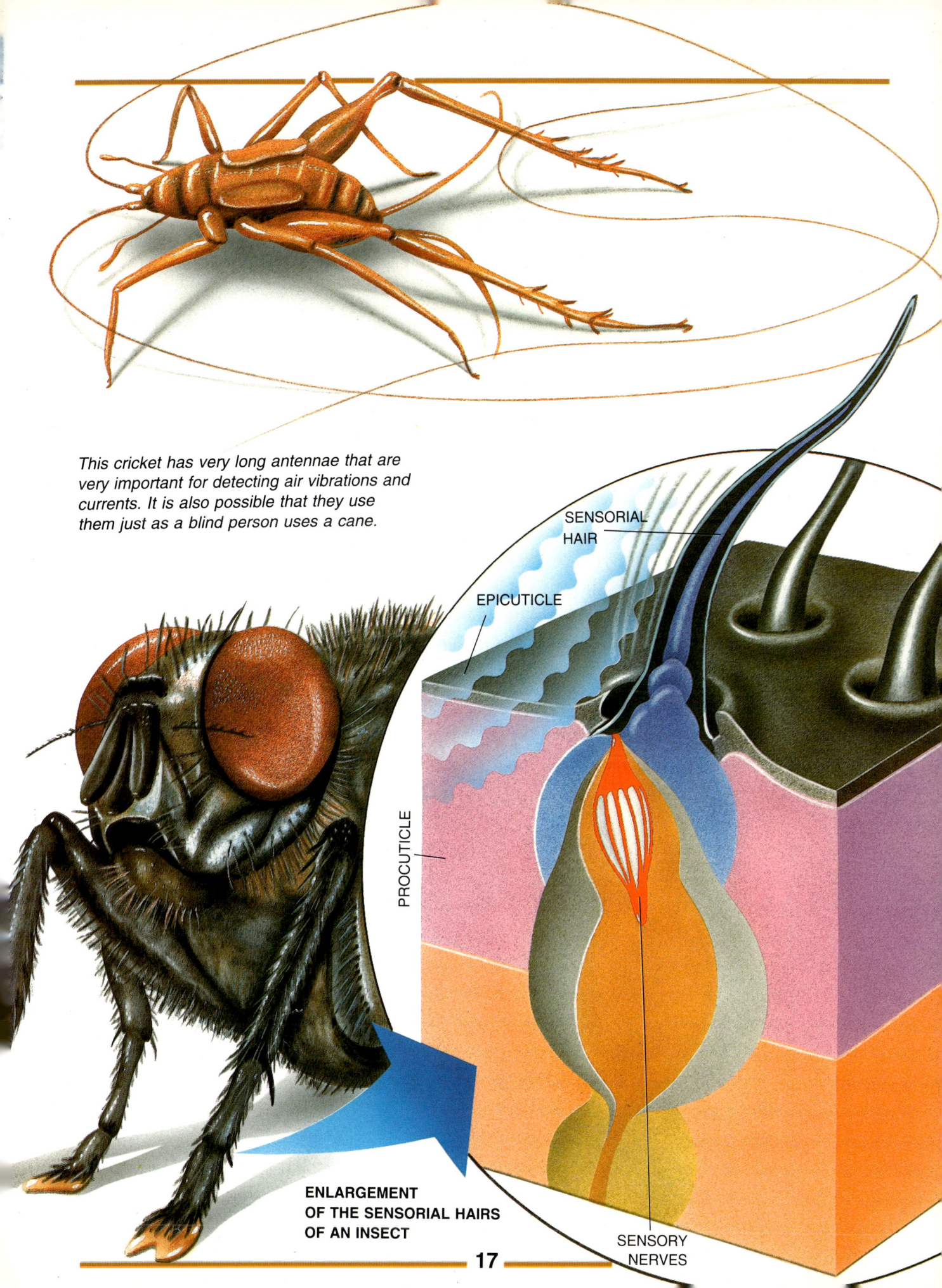

This cricket has very long antennae that are very important for detecting air vibrations and currents. It is also possible that they use them just as a blind person uses a cane.

SENSORIAL HAIR

EPICUTICLE

PROCUTICLE

ENLARGEMENT OF THE SENSORIAL HAIRS OF AN INSECT

SENSORY NERVES

Arthropod Skin

Do flies, spiders, and crabs have skin?

Arthropods make up 80 percent of all the known animal species in the world. One of the reasons for their great success is precisely their skin, or cuticle.

The cuticle has many different functions. It serves as a skeleton, protects the arthropod's body and extremities, and in some insects, serves as wings. One of the cuticle's most important functions is preventing loss of water or dehydration. Millions of years ago, arthropods were able to move from aquatic to terrestrial life because of this cuticle.

If you look carefully, you will notice that not all arthropods have the same hard cuticle. Some arthropods have a very soft shell while others have a very rigid one (like crabs and beetles).

There is, however, one problem with this very special type of skin. If the animal wants to grow, it has to be able to change its armor for a larger one. These periodic changes are absolutely necessary because the arthropod's shell has to be the same size as the growing body inside.

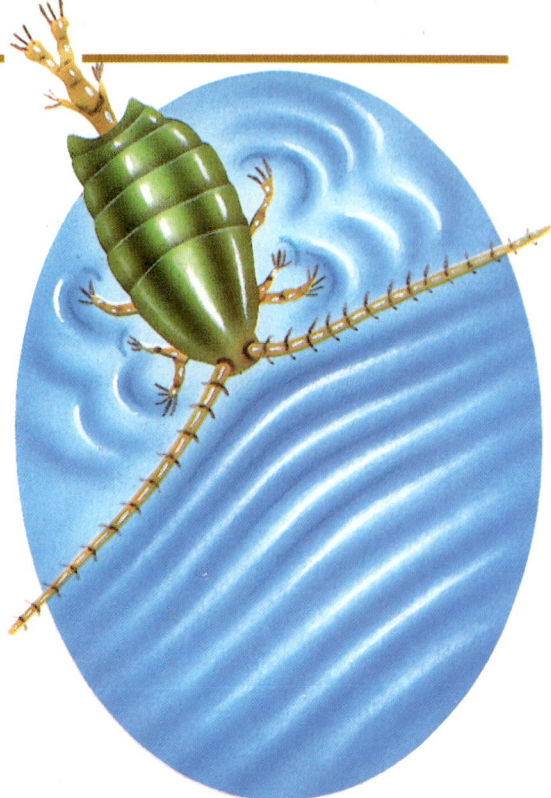

Copepods are very small crustaceans. They swim by propelling themselves with large antennules, or feelers, which also work like sensitive organs because of the large amount of sensorial hairs on them.

Some species of crabs can change their shell up to eight times just in their first year. Afterward, they continue changing their shells once or twice a year. Everything is changed including their sensitive antennae.

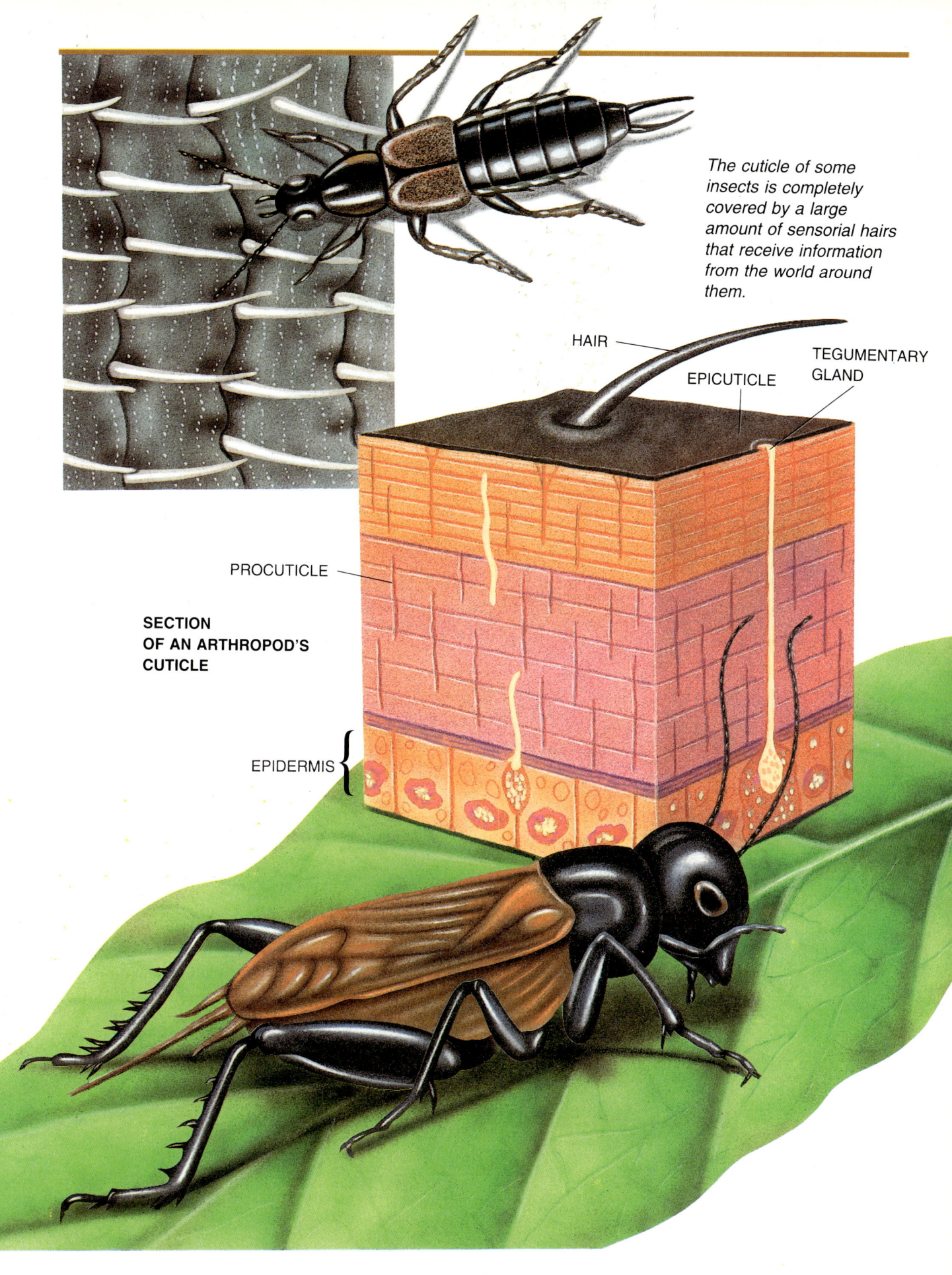

Sensitive Whiskers

Have you ever noticed that a single animal can have different kinds of hair?

Think about all the different kinds of hair that are on an animal's head, tail, eyelashes, and in its nostrils. Each of these different types of hair have been evolving and specializing themselves for one specific function.

Among mammals, there is a very special type of hair that serves as a receptor for the sense of touch: the whiskers. They are on many mammals' snouts. Whiskers are especially developed in nocturnal mammals.

Whiskers are made up of tactile nerve endings that are only found at the hair's root and at the base of hair follicles. These hairs are incredibly sensitive due to the presence of several nerve endings at the roots. These roots are shaped like caverns and look like the skin of erectile tissue. There are other types of *hair follicles* that also have many nerve endings but are less sensitive than whiskers because they do not have any cavernous structures associated with them.

When something stimulates the whisker, the increase in blood pressure in these structures is transmitted to the root, stimulating the whisker's sensitive nerves. That information is then sent to the brain for interpretation.

Seals are extraordinary fishers even in completely dark waters. The secret behind their success is the hairs on their chin that are very sensitive to touch. They can even detect the small aquatic waves a fish makes while swimming.

The otter's whiskers are very sensitive and of great use.

The duckbill platypus (left) can look for food underwater with its eyes closed thanks to its beak, which is a very special organ. Not only is it sensitive to touch but it can also detect the electrical discharges that the prawns it feeds on emit. Prawns produce electrical fields of less than one thousandth of a volt, but the duckbill can detect them from more than 3 feet away.

A feline's whiskers help it measure the distance between itself and nearby objects thus avoiding crashing into them.

The hippopotamus has sensitive hairs that help it detect the presence of nearby objects in the muddy waters.

The Sand Scorpions' Touch

The sand scorpion is a nocturnal hunter. It is a primitive arthropod that lacks the more developed senses of sight, hearing, and smell, which other predators use to find their prey.

The sand scorpion cannot see nor hear the insects it feeds on; it has to rely on its receptors that are extremely sensitive to even the smallest vibrations in the sand.

When a moth lands on the sand near a scorpion, the scorpion quickly runs toward its prey. It rarely fails in these attacks. Scientists believe that these animals do not respond to visual or auditory stimuli but that they can detect the mechanical vibrations in the sand and learn from these the precise information needed to find their prey. The scorpion is even capable of finding prey hiding underground.

When night falls, the scorpion leaves its den and waits in ambush for its prey to come close enough to attack. If the scorpion is not successful, it can keep itself immobile for hours before returning to its den.

When prey enters the hunting area, the scorpion puts itself into alert position. It opens its *pedipalpi* and extends them forward while lifting its body up off the sand. The scorpion turns its pedipalpi quickly and advances a few inches. If the pedipalpi manage to touch its prey, the scorpion stays still until the prey moves again.

Ladybug larvae have very poor eyesight, and so in order to hunt, they go from stem to stem, feeling and touching every corner until they find their prey, such as these plant lice.

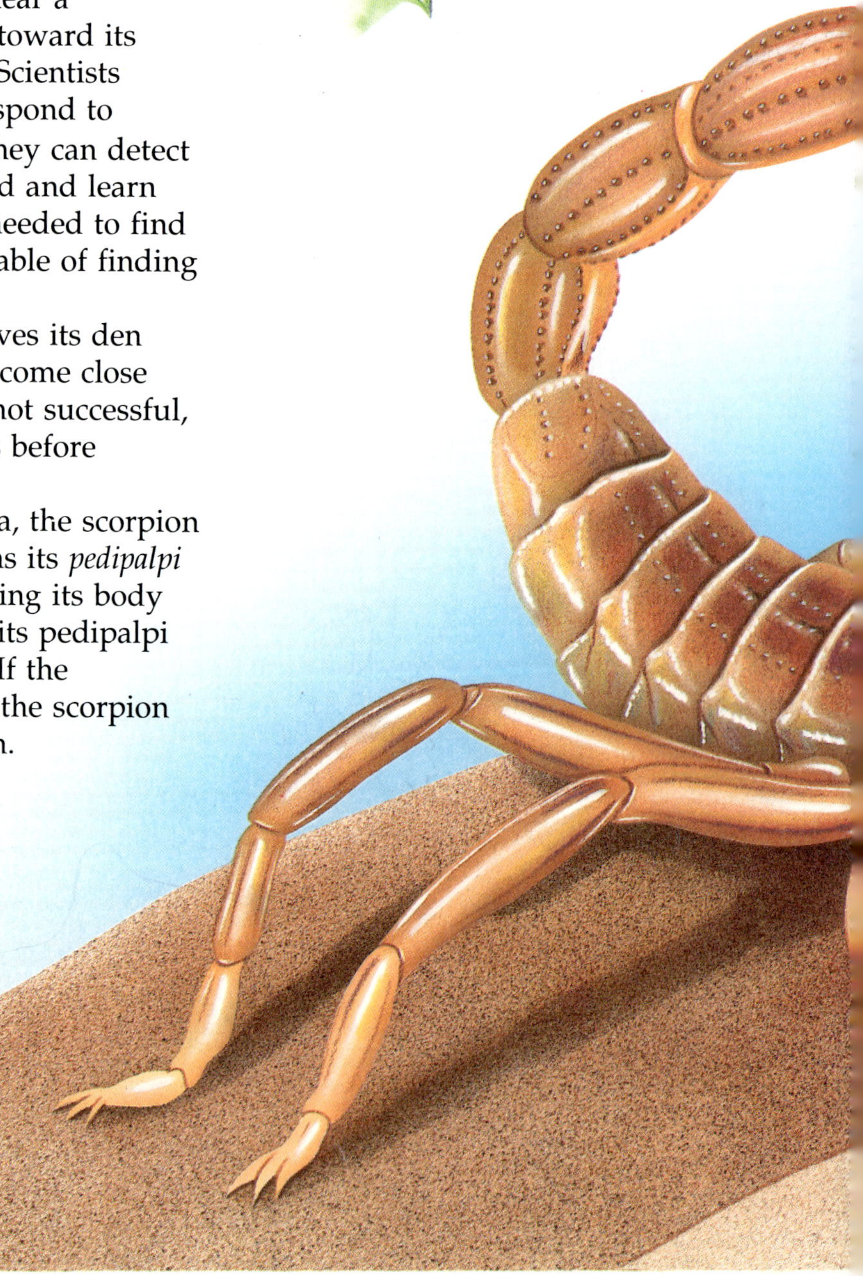

The sand scorpion can detect a cockroach digging from as far away as 3 feet. The scorpion slowly approaches and lifts up its hind part. It jabs at the sand several times with its pedipalpi until touching and grabbing the cockroach.

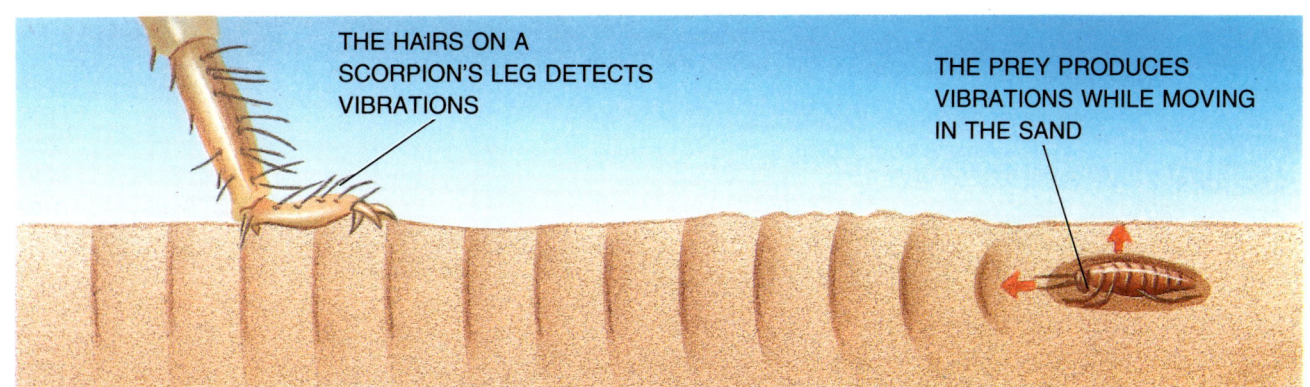

THE HAIRS ON A SCORPION'S LEG DETECTS VIBRATIONS

THE PREY PRODUCES VIBRATIONS WHILE MOVING IN THE SAND

The sensitive hairs on the scorpion's legs are extremely important for its detection mechanism. To find its prey, it compares the signals it receives from the different detectors on its legs.

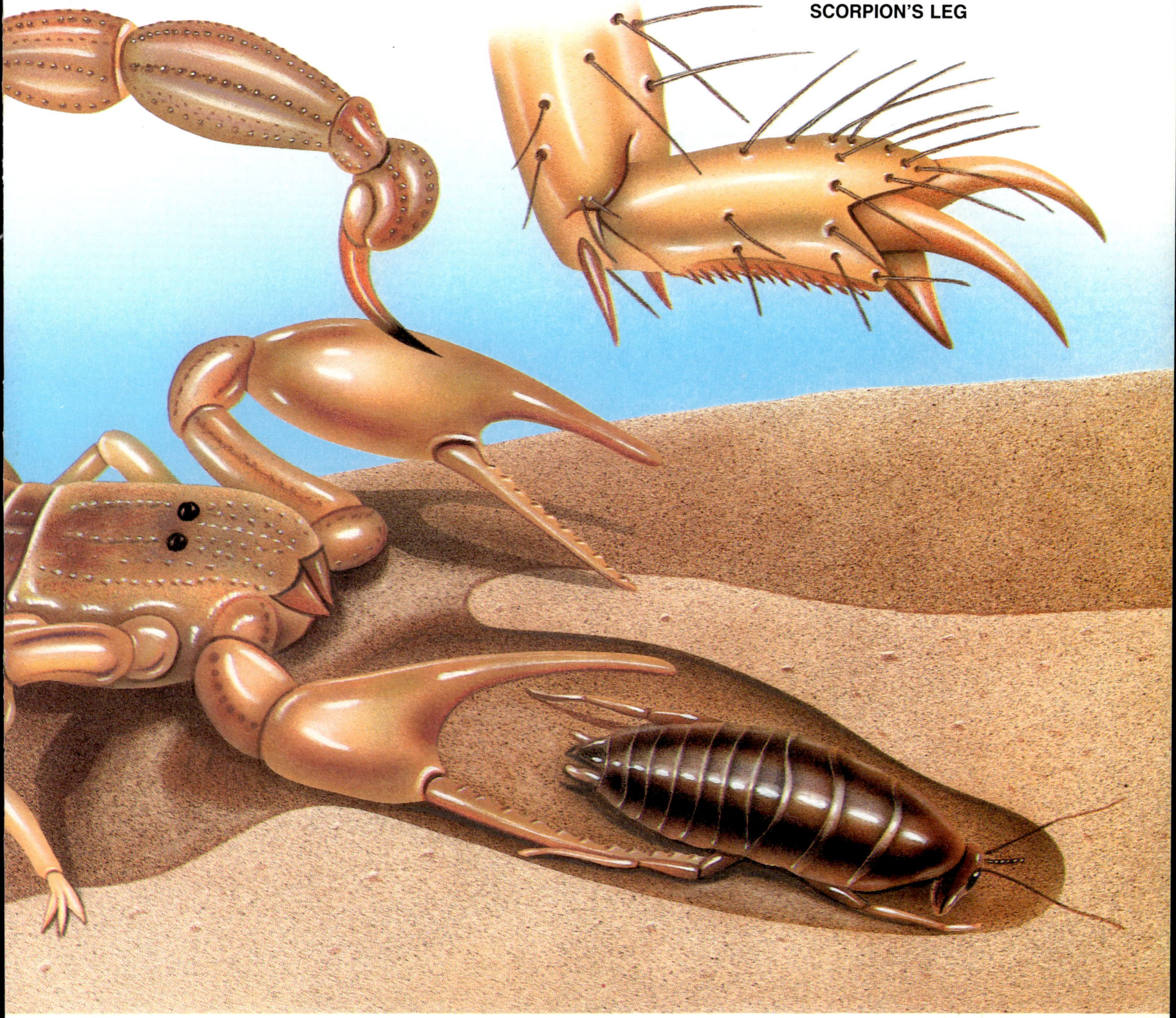

ENLARGEMENT OF A SCORPION'S LEG

Sensitive to the Force of Gravity

Sensitivity to the force of gravity is very common among animals because it gives them very useful information about what is above and below them.

The more complex animals have gravity receptors known as statocysts. These receptors are made up of a type of small particle or little stone of calcium carbonate that lays against several sensitive hairs. When the animal moves, any of its body's movements relative to the force of gravity cause the stone to move and stimulate the *cilia* of other sensitive cells that quickly send the information to the central nervous system.

Acceleration is also detected in a similar way—in this case, liquid is moved. This liquid moves the little hairs in the direction that the animal is moving. In vertebrates, the organ responsible for this is the inner ear. It consists of three semicircular canals that are positioned in three different planes all perpendicular to one another. These canals are full of liquid and any body movement moves the liquid, which stimulates the sensitive cells.

"Upside down information" is very important for many animals. Cats, for example, are capable of turning their bodies around in midair, always landing on their feet. What quick reflexes!

For flying animals it is especially important to constantly control their position relative to the hard ground below them.

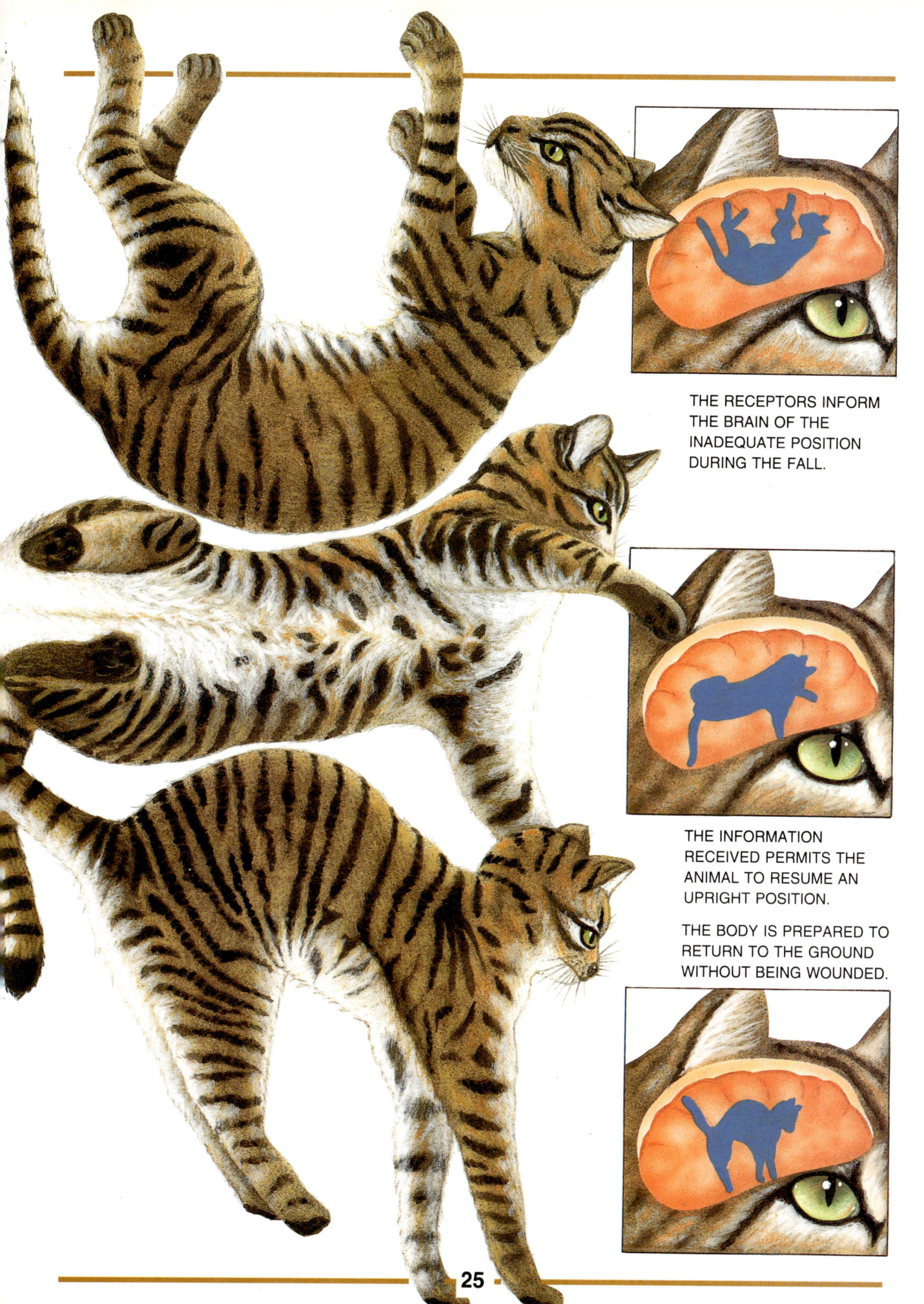

THE RECEPTORS INFORM THE BRAIN OF THE INADEQUATE POSITION DURING THE FALL.

THE INFORMATION RECEIVED PERMITS THE ANIMAL TO RESUME AN UPRIGHT POSITION.

THE BODY IS PREPARED TO RETURN TO THE GROUND WITHOUT BEING WOUNDED.

Other Special Sensitivities

In the animal world, there are many other types of senses that are difficult to include among the five senses that you know about.

Did you know that there is a large number of bacteria that is capable of moving around by guiding themselves by the earth's *magnetic field*? Inside these cells, you can find crystals made of magnetite (a strong magnetic mineral found underground). In some bacteria, these crystals form an almost lineal chain that works as if it were a compass needle. The bacteria's magnetic orientation is called magnetotaxy. There are other animals, like the shark, which can also detect small changes in the magnetic field. But there are also other animals that are very sensitive to air currents. It is logical to assume that birds and flying insects are tuned into the changes in air currents because they can affect their ability to fly.

Scientists have discovered that the locust's antennae are its speedometer. As the locust increases its speed, the air resistance increases and bends the antennae further and further back. The scorpion is one of the animals most sensitive to air currents. The delicate hairs on its claws detect extremely small air movements provoked by insects as they move around the scorpion.

Every locust can calculate its speed due to the air passing over its antennae. This way they can adjust their flight to move around together with minimal effort.

Snakes keep their entire body constantly touching the ground and are very sensitive to even the slightest vibration, including the ones that precede an earthquake. Long ago, snakes were thought to be magical because it was said that they "knew" when an earthquake was about to hit.

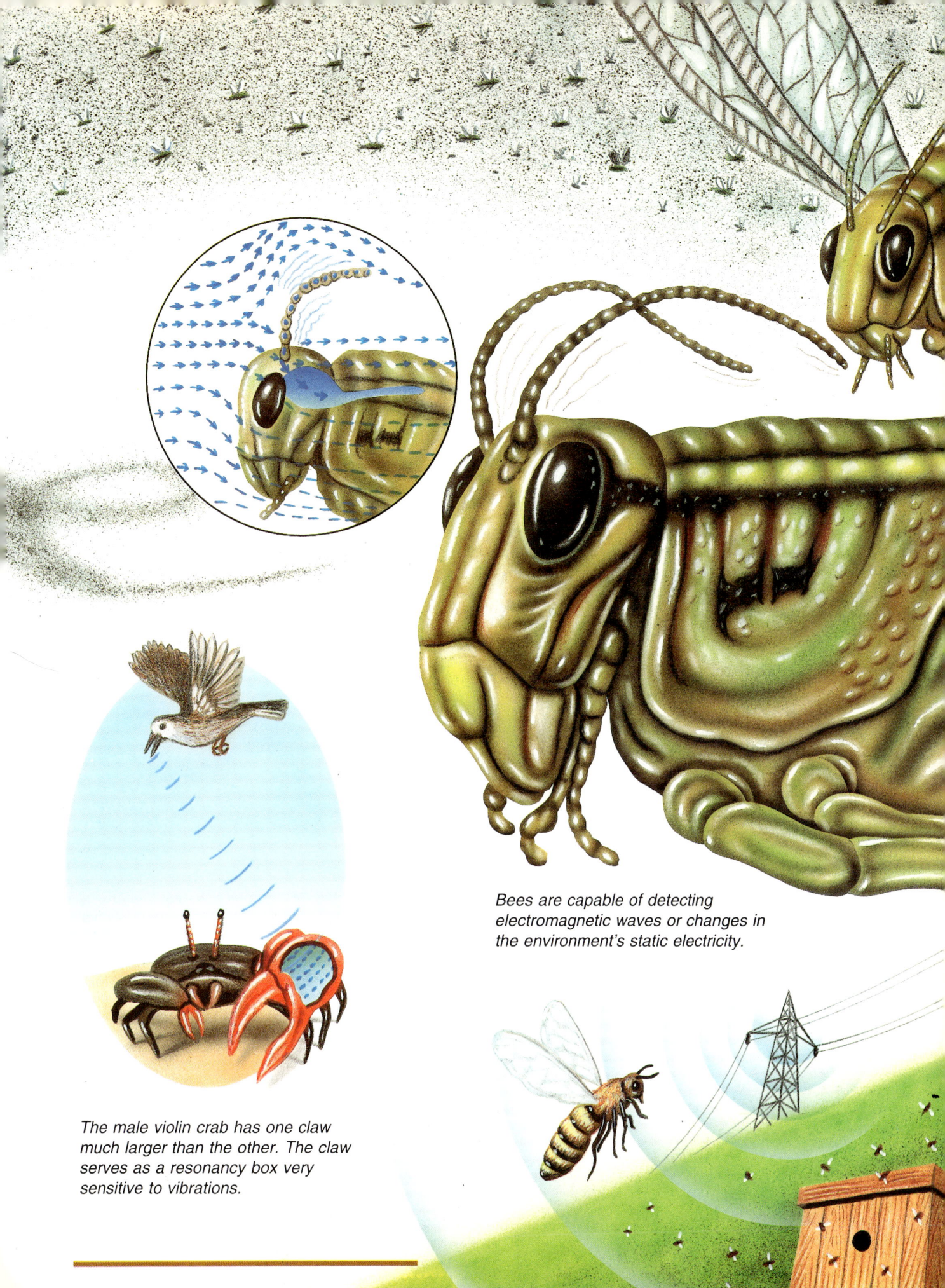

Bees are capable of detecting electromagnetic waves or changes in the environment's static electricity.

The male violin crab has one claw much larger than the other. The claw serves as a resonancy box very sensitive to vibrations.

How Spiders Detect Their Prey

Spiders have a highly developed sense of touch.

Just like the sand scorpion, the spider guides itself toward its victims by "listening" to its victim's movements, using its legs. Spiders also have a sensing ability in their pedipalpi.

Spiders are one of the few animals that are capable of making and setting traps to hunt. These are the well-known spiderwebs that, while appearing to be very fragile, are in reality mortal traps for other insects. Many spiders base their conduct on their ability to make silk threads that have many different uses such as the construction of spiderwebs and bags to carry their eggs.

Spiders have to be attentive in order to detect a victim that has fallen onto the web. If the spider is not paying attention, the prey could escape and damage the web that took the spider much effort to build. Often, the spider waits in the center of the web to attack, but in some cases the spider hangs a thread from the web's center to its hiding place. The spider keeps one of its legs on this thread so it can immediately detect the vibrations on its web.

The most important information a spider gets always comes from its web. Some scientists believe that the spider can interpret what exactly is causing the movements on its silk threads even before the spider advances toward its prey.

The terrifying ant lion larvae bury themselves underground and build a funnel-shaped trap. At the bottom of the funnel their jaws stick out, waiting for a victim to fall down the slopes. Sometimes, they even throw sand at their prey to make them fall.

1. The trap-door spider hides in its tunnel with only its legs sticking out to detect the approaching prey's vibrations.

2. When the hairs on its legs feel an insect's vibrations, the spider opens the trapdoor and attacks its victim.

3. It then drags the immobile victim's body toward the tunnel where it hides again, this time to enjoy its lunch.

A spider always keeps one of its sensitive legs on its web so that it can feel the vibrations its prey make when they get trapped. It is very important for the spider to immobilize its victims quickly because they could break the web and escape.

The spider's feelers are responsible for its sense of smell, taste, and touch.

FEELERS

29

The Electrical Sense

Did you know that there are animals capable of generating animal electricity?

These electrical organs can be found in hundreds of salt and freshwater fish species but, in reality, only a few are actually capable of emitting a strong charge. These organs consist of nerve and muscle cells that have undergone great change.

The ability to emit strong electrical charges is an incredible defense mechanism and a valuable tool for capturing prey without hardly moving. The stingray, or torpedo, and the electrical eel from South America have the most powerful electrical organs of all. Both species are capable of generating electrical charges measuring from 50 to even more than 200 volts.

The animal electrical organs are made up of small electrical plates, called electrocites, that overlap one another forming columns. Each plate contains various layers of specialized cells that charge themselves instantly once they get the order through the nerves to produce an electrical discharge.

There are also a lot of fish capable of detecting small differences in the electrical field around them. The rays, for example, are the most sensitive of all to electricity. They take advantage of the small charges that their victims emit to help them find their prey when they launch their terrifying final attack.

The electrical fish constantly emit small electrical charges in the water around them. Thanks to the waves that these make, they can detect if any object penetrates the electrical field. It is very useful at night and in muddy rivers.

ELECTROPLATES

The electrical organs can be found on different parts of the body, depending on the species.

The electrical organs tend to be used for defensive and hunting purposes. Here you can see how the torpedo captures its food. It stuns its prey with an electrical charge that lets it take its time attacking and devouring it.

FEB 1996